THE
WINDOW

THE WINDOW
a portal to my innermost thoughts

SADIE DUNBAR

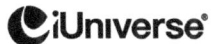

THE WINDOW
A PORTAL TO MY INNERMOST THOUGHTS

Copyright © 2024 Sadie Dunbar.

All rights reserved. No part of this book may be used or reproduced by any means, graphic, electronic, or mechanical, including photocopying, recording, taping or by any information storage retrieval system without the written permission of the author except in the case of brief quotations embodied in critical articles and reviews.

iUniverse books may be ordered through booksellers or by contacting:

iUniverse
1663 Liberty Drive
Bloomington, IN 47403
www.iuniverse.com
844-349-9409

Because of the dynamic nature of the Internet, any web addresses or links contained in this book may have changed since publication and may no longer be valid. The views expressed in this work are solely those of the author and do not necessarily reflect the views of the publisher, and the publisher hereby disclaims any responsibility for them.

Any people depicted in stock imagery provided by Getty Images are models, and such images are being used for illustrative purposes only. Certain stock imagery © Getty Images.

ISBN: 978-1-6632-6166-3 (sc)
ISBN: 978-1-6632-6167-0 (e)

Library of Congress Control Number: 2024906168

Print information available on the last page.

iUniverse rev. date: 04/11/2024

To the ones that broke me in the first place,
to the one that helped me grow again,
and to the one that helped me thrive at my best.

"Words have no power to impress the mind without the exquisite horror of their reality."
Edgar Allan Poe

Contents

Foreword xi

Outside the Window 1
The Striped Dress 5
Shower Curtain 9
Superman 11
Chocolate 14
CD 17
Monster 19
No Relief 22
Juicy Fruit 25
Appointment 27
Dreams 31
Mercy 33
Daughter of a Pisces 35
Complex 36
Genuine 39
Quicksand 42
Yours Truly, ... 44

About the Author 47

Foreword

This book consists of poetry written over five or so years. During that time, life around me fast-forwarded and I felt stuck in place. In my head I strung along words until I created beautifully, broken poems; words that were trapped and the only way out was through this. There is a vulnerability in letting those thoughts and feelings out for just anyone to pick up and read. It is this vulnerability that I am entrusting to you as the readers. Please note that there are two sides to every story. My version is not the only one. With that, I present to you The Window.

Outside the Window

Even though the birds are singing,
the sky fills with stygian grey clouds
thunderous,
Pregnant with the downpour that promises to water the planet.

It is at this moment I'm losing myself,
staring beyond the window to the world outside.
because I am trapped behind the glass
and no matter how much
I try to convince myself that the rain is not coming,

I know that I am wrong.
I am kidding myself,
conditioning myself
to believe that if it does rain.
if it floods us out of our home,
we won't survive.
They say that I am exaggerating.
but I know it is true.

I shouldn't think so negatively.
I must pretend that the rain doesn't bother me
even if it does.

My head hurts-
and the pinging of water droplets

ricochet around the inside of my skull
bouncing back and forth.
The sound draws my attention back to the window,
the window that shows me the world outside.

The glisten of rain on the window
glares as the cars that pass by shine their headlights;
magnifying the water's shadow reflected on the wall.
I stand there looking, searching...
when will this stop?
The constant fretting,
the constant pressure?
It's not the kind that turns coal into diamonds;

the kind that crushed Atlas
as he held the weight of the world on his shoulders.

I stand and take one last look out into the storm.
It is raging,
the storm that I was preparing for.
I knew I was right.

There is nothing more I can do but pull the drapes and shut it out.
cut myself out of the picture,
close the portal-
the window that shows me the world outside.

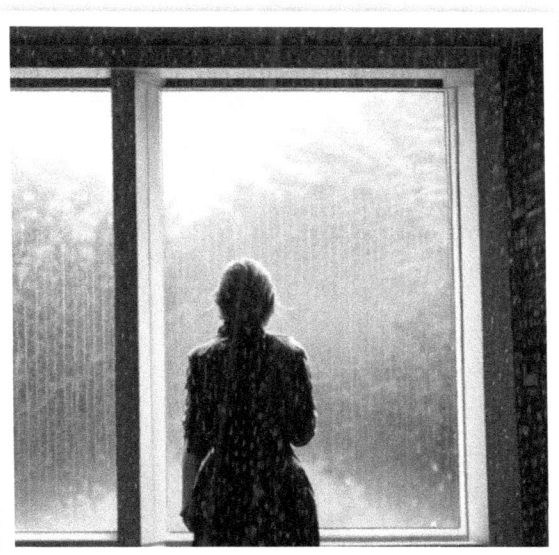

The Striped Dress

It is not often that I feel comfortable in my own skin.
I usually feel anxious,
scared that my assets will not reach
the unattainable standards that are in place;
I feel their eyes follow me;
it can only mean that they are judging me,
they are criticizing any confidence I may have in myself.

There are some days I shed my skin,
to feel confident, despite the constant fear
of never being enough.
On those days, I pull the striped dress
out from the back of my closet

When I wear it, I feel full.
I am floating a foot above the ground.
where my insecurities cannot drown me.
A girl I pass on the street
disguises a look of pain upon seeing me.
but it isn't me.
that she is seeing.
It's my dress.

The insecurities that had momentarily diminished return,
as my confidence leaves my body
and transfers to the girl,
whom I sympathize with

That is the problem with this world.
We are constantly criticized for simply being,
our darkest secrets hidden away.
Like how we alter our appearance to please a man.

Not all girls have a striped dress.
And so I shed my newfound skin,
leave myself publicly exposed
to give this girl a glimmer of hope;
that one day she will feel free enough
to repay the swan for her down feather coat.

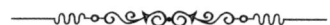

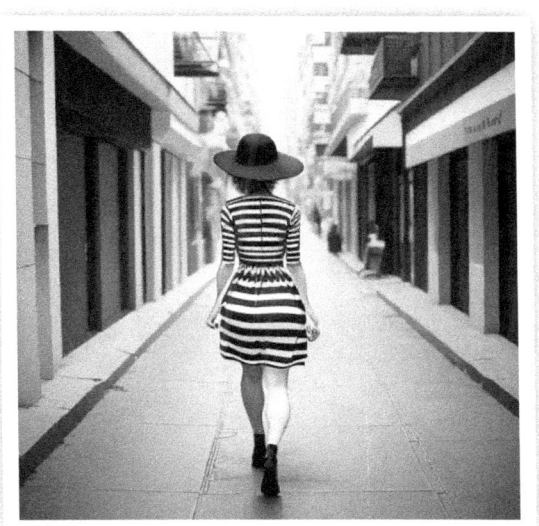

Shower Curtain

Why is it that I can't bring myself,
to the point of stripping?
To take off every layer that covers my skin,
until I am bare?

Then I have to reach in and
turn the water on,
making sure it's the temperature of fire.

There I must stand and wait
until I can slide my body into the stream of flames,
feel them envelope me,
my skin turning pink and splotchy.

I force my arms into motion,
mechanically going about
the routine
of cleaning myself.

I stare blankly at the shower curtain.

No matter how I scour my skin,
the inky shadow looms over me,
attached at my hip,
an enemy that follows me everywhere I go.

Some days he hides away
in the back pocket of my jeans.
But lately he has been curled around my brain
infiltrating my senses.

I turn off the water,
feeling a little better.
but once I dry myself off and pull back the shower curtain
the better is lost.

Superman

I once saw you,
as a hero.
You had painted a picture for me,
and only me to see.

The thing is,
you forgot to put away the paint
and even if it took me years
I see now you're not the painter,
I once thought you to be.

Just a scared little boy
crying his way home to mommy.
You couldn't be a man
But rather step back and
let the new woman take the reins.

There goes one!
You get one more chance
but instead of stepping up,
you let her fill your fucking head.

With lies and delusions,
things she wants only you to see.
Much the same way you painted
a picture for the daughter long gone.

Now you have none.
The hero you are unbecoming.
You are no Superman,
not even a man,

You have done it all wrong.

Chocolate

Your lips were sweet,
they dripped with honey
All the lies and promises
You just couldn't bring yourself to keep them.
The words that escape have gone sour.

Your tongue was candy,
melting in my mouth
as you devour me.
until it becomes sharper than a blade
mocking me
and belittling me.
but I thought I was "all you could ever want"?

Your skin is salt
The balance
the missing x in the equation

Yet,
the flavor of you
could not mask the
taste
of your bitter dark chocolate heart.

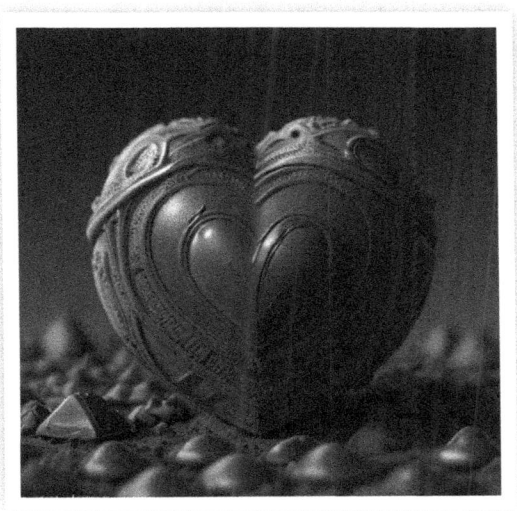

CD

Cassettes were always easy.
Pull the tape and you just
need to wind it back up again.

But you are not so simple.

We worry whether
or not
you will get scratched
or snapped in half.

We worry about the marring of
your rainbow gleam,
the unblemished masterpiece.

You darling
are turning vintage.
They can get what you offer from
countless other sources.
without the hassle
of maintaining perfection.

Know your worth.

Monster

The camera on my phone is open
and I look through the lens
to the reflection in the mirror.
Instead of doe eyes and an hourglass figure,
I see a creature staring back at me.

It is not me in the glass,
not me in that post I put on Instagram
It is not my picture.

That must be why people don't like it,
why they don't comment
with beautiful praise.
It must be because I have been replaced with
the deepest darkest horrors.
That has to be the reason.

Before I snapped the picture,
I felt elated,
joyous.
Because for once I saw a queen in the mirror

She posed the right way,
with her hair fanned around her shoulders.
She winked at herself,

eyelashes fluttering as the shutter of the camera clicked.

She sought to make others see
the beauty she had found
within herself.

But now in her place
stands a monster,
seven feet tall.
With grizzled lips,
and fangs protruding out from its mouth.
Instead of beauty, I see ugly.
I see the beast that lives under my skin.

I see the way the world sees me;
a monster.

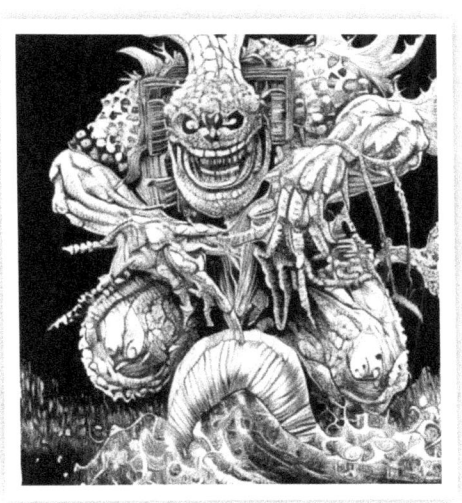

No Relief

Losing you was hard,
the hardest thing I have ever endured.
My chest felt like it was caving in.
"That feeling will go away", they assured.
but they were wrong.
I still feel empty and alone.
Losing you was more than losing your body and soul.
I lost the person that was my home.
It has been a year and some months now,
but the weight has not yet lifted.
There is a cavity in my chest
and my vital organs have shifted.
I cannot decide whether it is guilt or grief.
The reason I feel these feelings and have found no relief.

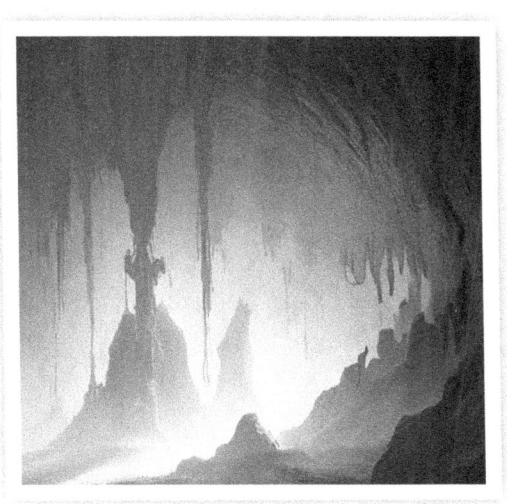

Juicy Fruit

There were only four grandchildren,
two of which were thrust upon her
with no regard to the fact that
she may want to enjoy
her golden years.

The youngest was there when it happened,
the event that brings us here today;
celebrating the life she lived.

The second youngest is just spoiled and sheltered.
I really shouldn't put any blame on her
she did her best
with kids that were her flesh and blood
but they weren't her kids.

The second oldest she was in a tough spot
the middle child
always feared
that she wouldn't measure up

The eldest - who got the call on a late shift -
She screamed herself to sleep
after a canyon of tears
but no amount of crying

could fill the gaping hole
that broke open in her chest.

Because her life was so much more than her legacy.
I'll never be able to chew another stick of Juicy Fruit again.

Appointment

They tell you a time
when you should be there
and don't you dare be late
or they will refuse to see you

But what they don't know is
the reason I missed my appointment
was because I was holding her hand
as she took her last breath

I was crying in my car
trying to pull myself together
wishing to God (if he is up there)
to ease my pain and dull my suffering

I was having a breakdown
gasping for air
over the thought of yanking myself out of the car
walking into the building

I'm sitting in that godforsaken waiting room
for the vultures to circle me
stare
judge.

You look up at me over your horn-rimmed glasses
Smacking your gum like I am insignificant to you.
You tell me the doctor will see me
When he is free.

uncomfortable plastic chairs
a magazine
I flip through the pages for half
an hour or more

And I think until my memories grow dark.
To when she came into the room like a missile
all because I took lip-gloss to school
The lesson learned in fury.

What a whore I was
in the third grade
when all I wanted
was to be cool.

That is the reason I need to see the doctor
It's because my past haunts me
my memories play
on a loop in my head.

of everything that has happened to me
of everything that I deem unimportant
of everything that has shaped me into me
of everything I have repressed to survive.

The things that scare away my slumber dreams.

Dreams

There are days
when I wake up from awful dreams
Not nightmares
nothing bad happens

But I see life when it was simpler.
When I had friends
people to spend all my free time with
I wake up in tears

because my birthday was last Sunday
and not a single person wished me a good one
Not one reaches out when I'm at my lowest
No one at all

I feel so damn lonely
and fucked up
that I cry
the tears hitting the barrier of my eyelashes
then trailing down my cheeks
ice cold

I wonder when
I will have a dream
That is worth dreaming

Mercy

I didn't think I would see the day
when my parents were no longer my parents
Instead, strangers,
passing through my life and picking apart every piece of me they could
obsessing over everything I did and saying it bad
I was the worst daughter my dad could imagine having
I learned what it meant to become a disappointment long before I knew the word.
It started before they locked me out of the house
(though they think it sounds better to say I just never came home)
I slept that night in the break room at work.
collected pity like a pocket of pennies pulled out of a water fountain.
I hated every pathetic moment that passed by
where people looked at me with pitiful eyes.
I scrounged money. Savings depleted to pay for an apartment that stood over a dingy bar
Looking back, I didn't realize how dangerous it was
Didn't think of the damage it would cause me.
I finally decided to face the music of their decision
When they made it seem like it was mine
I collected my stuff from my room at their house

Which they so kindly packed for me
They burned my bed.
I slept on an air mattress for months.
Do you know how hard it was for a girl
Living alone
Working at Mcdonalds
Out of high school for only a week
To pay for an apartment?
I prayed that eventually I would be given
A reprieve from the relentless revenge I received from
People who recited lines from a book
Trying to remind me
That they "loved" me.
To this day I have yet to be granted mercy.

Daughter of a Pisces

I learned early on that promises of commitment can be broken just as easily as they are made. It did not matter that I was blood. Their lives moved on the second I was gone. It was the start of a mistake. I'm a lifelong regret that acted as a pawn in a much bigger game.

I wonder at times if there is any love left at all. Or did it empty like a giant cavern, sucking the dregs of affection deep into a chasm that sits between us?

At the age of twenty-five, I realized it mattered not that I was someone's daughter, You would tear me apart until I felt nothing. My nerve endings numb from the trauma of being severed so brutally. I should have known that it was too good to be true.

If only you had been born just a few days before maybe we would have had a chance.

Complex

There was never any doubt that from the beginning.
We knew
this would either end in forever
or the worst heartbreak that we've ever known.

We were tested time and time again
and we thought we were ahead of the storm;
too far out of its reach to be caught up in the crosswinds.

But here we are staring death right in the face;
the reaper has chosen this time to be more than a test.
Can we out run Hades himself? Or should we surrender the white flag?

The complexities of how this will go
pile up in front of my eyes.
A million different situations and outcomes each with its own list of pros and cons

What will happen to our dogs? The bed?
The things in the house that were once ours?
Who do they belong to now?

I loved you with every fiber of my being
And I pushed myself too far in thinking that I could change
Or maybe hoping you would too

But I am so very tired.

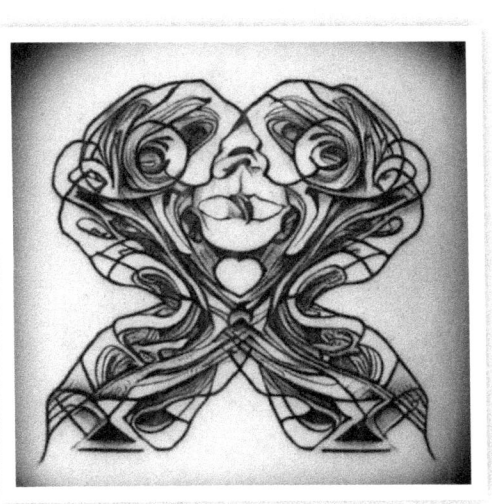

Genuine

Do not mistake me for someone,
so gullible,
they cannot differentiate
between a smokescreen
and an honest compliment.

I know you have it all-
the perfect family,
the perfect life.
Nothing can disrupt your peaceful little world

but you have all the power,
to destroy another person
for shits and giggles
because you can.

So when you approach me
and tell me that
my "hair looks nice today"
or that you like how I put on my makeup

I know that you are gaslighting me
Covering up an insult with a pretty, satin bow

But, I know
you are incapable
of saying anything genuine
unless it benefits you -

Quicksand

I medicate
to normalize my brain waves
and untie all the knots that prevent
my endorphins from going where they need to.

But sometimes it doesn't do the job
I am stuck in the pit-
black goo filling the hole around me.
and my feet are cemented in the ground-
stopping me from loosening myself -

Yours Truly,

Today is the day that I complete my metamorphosis;
They say it requires time to rewire life again
and yes maybe it will;
I am in the strangest of places,
not quite between a rock and a hard place,
but more-so stuck on a strip of sand dividing oceans.

I am stepping out of my seven year incubation period;
I have nothing but love for the past -
for without it, I would not be who I am today
I will forever be grateful for you and love you.

Always in my heart, no matter how your feelings have shifted,
you will always be a part of me regardless.
But it's time for this chapter to end;
Let the celebrations start
as you step into your new self.

Yours Truly,
Sadie.

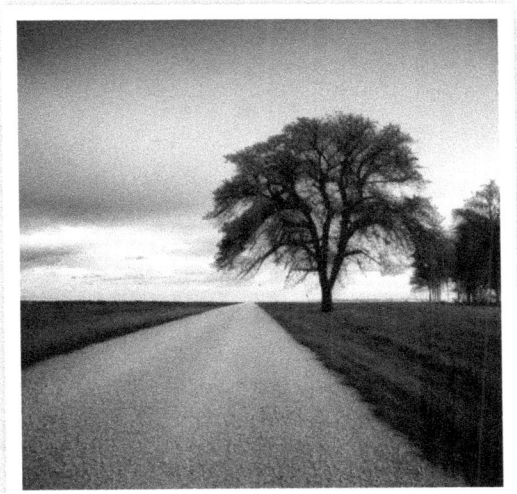

About the Author

Sadie Dunbar is a full time student at SNHU and a full time medication technician. Between the many busy hours she finds time here and there to write poetry to share with the world in hopes of finding likeminded people that can grow and connect with her writing.

www.ingramcontent.com/pod-product-compliance
Lightning Source LLC
Chambersburg PA
CBHW070830220526
45466CB00002B/790